Section 1   UNDERSTAND

DYSFUNCTION

Understanding the development of emotional dysfunction requires a thorough understanding of Attitude and Expectations. Furthermore, changes in emotional dysfunction can be made only by adding new alternatives to our belief system. This can done by creating new Engrams, which are active memory routines, within our bank of subconscious beliefs and activity templates. Our life's memory bank contains records of every activity, belief, physical routine, and experiences which number in the millions. The subconscious mind forgets nothing.

Incidents inscribed with only small emotional content are only lightly etched in memory. Experiences with strong emotion are deeply ingrained into the subconscious mind.

In contrast, the conscious mind which creates original thoughts and directs management to the subconscious mind, is very puny in comparison. Also the conscious mind is entirely temporary, while the subconscious mind is permanent and retains a complete record. The conscious mind has an effective duration of only a few minutes, then these directives are gone forever. Consequently the subconscious mind again resumes full management of the total body.

All programming and reprogramming of the subconscious mind

involves vivid sensory imagery generated by the conscious mind. This vivid imagery requires one or more of the senses to build the formation of new Engrams which will forever reside in the subconscious mind. Our subconscious mind can simultaneously program millions and millions of finite details for the complete execution of the Engram desired.

The two keys tools which are managed by the conscious mind and that can manage changes in the subconscious mind are <u>Attitude</u> and <u>Expectations</u>. The managing imagery that we create must use one or more of the body's senses expressed through attitude and expectation.

The five senses of sight, hearing, smell, touch and taste keep us oriented physically to our environment. Our sixth sense Attitude is the all-important sense that keeps us engaged with another person or animal. Attitude is like ever-active radar because it is constantly sending and receiving informational signals. This sending is an ongoing process to keep us oriented with other individuals.

Inherently, through intuition (the seventh sense) we are capable of understanding accurately our reality of the moment. Also if we choose, we can be aware whether or not the other person is paying attention and is tuned into us. If we pay further attention, we can be aware when the other person drifts off and is no longer in touch with us. All relationship we have with other people is the constant process of reading Attitude between them and us. If either person is out of similar realities, then you have a situation of active emotional dysfunction.

Any time that we make a move or thought that is out of reality, which means wanting something to be different from actually what is occurring at this moment, then we reap miserable consequences in the form of unwanted emotions - minor or major hell on earth - and suffering. On the other hand, if the action or thought is seen as precisely what was destined to happen, then we are in the comfort of reality. We within ourselves are the only one to create peace and contentment. In this way, we alone are the authors of our emotional life.

To always be in reality there is one very strict unalterable rule, that is, that we are totally responsible for our emotions. Only change in our expectations can adjust the consequences for our feelings. Nobody can make us feel anything. However we can create local conditions and circumstances, wherein it is likely to come to the conclusion that we hope would develop.

If we are not fully mature emotionally, then the problem is complicated because at all times we are simultaneously in two levels of reality, conscience and subconscious. The message we project is in our attitude and may not be the one for which we had hoped. The reality of our infantile childish belief behavior and the reality of this present day adult clash.   When we are completely mature in our emotional development, then the two realities are exactly the same. This concurrence of wisdom is the state of the legendary wise man at the top of the mountain - "Nirvana".   This is the ultimate evolution of the spirit, that state of bliss where our deepest emotional reality is identical with our conscious thought and action, releasing the full power of our personality at all times.

When we were born our brain and nervous system were already in place and functioning. However many of the nerves had not yet developed their insulating coating and the synapses were only partially hooked up and functioning. In the months after birth we rapidly began further development of our nervous system. In our second and third years we had great changes and by the end of the third year we even began to develop a conscience and to recognize the rights of other individuals. At ages 3 to 6 we learned how to deal effectively and respond to other individuals. We then continued development and refinement until the age of 30.

By nature of our unique DNA, individualism is our most certain and vital attribute. As a separate human we are each capable of the most complex actions and thinking but we vitally need a safe space and supporting environment in which to develop, free of outside directions which would distort normal maturation.   If our caretakers regarded us and supported us as *an entirely equal individual human* from the day that we were born, then we would naturally fulfill a great deal of our almost unlimited potential. Our Intellectual, physical and emotional growth would be most natural and complete.

Most parents, in their eagerness to make their children better individuals than they felt themselves to be, voluntarily take charge of their children's emotional development. Their guide for this training was only what had been passed down to them without improvement from their ancestors since time immemorial. Consequently all the emotional dysfunctions of the human race have been perpetuated for at least the ten thousand years of recorded history.

Most commonly parents, rather than treating their children as equals, look down upon them as possessions. Instead of supporting our natural growth, our caretakers likely treated us as if we were a pet dog or pony rather than a separate human being. With their very best of intentions for us, they attempted through their training to make us an emotionally better developed individual, free of the faults that they thought themselves to possess.

Many of the instructions from our caretakers were contrary to the fundamental evolutionary drive of our DNA. We instinctively resisted their pressure, which was in contradiction to our individuality. In an effort to resist the results of their harmful instructions, we responded spontaneously by developing entirely new Engrams as protective mechanisms to shield and block ourselves from the teaching of parental controlling demands.   Instinctively, by using our conscious mind, we employed <u>self hypnosis</u> to generate imagery designed to prompt our subconscious to create that new engrams.

When we generated these self-protecting suggestions, we automatically developed permanent arrest points (<u>hang ups</u>) in our natural emotional growth. These hang ups develop in a very emotional state and time. Also they are established at a highly specific point in the growth gradient of normal emotional development. The effects of these hang ups logically should have been temporary but all established Engrams are permanent.

In each Engram we also arrested our sense of reality for any thinking and action closely related to this specific incident. Each hang up continuously blocks the development of logic and reasoning. This new reality controls a whole category of related emotional evolution beyond that instant when the block is formed. These retrograde responses will be often repeated whenever we confront any similarly challenge. Our reality will be similar to any other infant or child. Even when we are re-enacting at a infantile level, our conscious mind will still hold the reality of us as an adult. We are then forced to choose which reality we want to display to others. This dichotomy of realities is a primary cause of <u>STRESS</u> in every individual.

Take an example: At twenty-four to thirty months of age we naturally have a limited scope of experience, knowledge and judgment, and so, consequentially, we command ourselves into conformity for doing, thinking and acting the same way over and over. Also at that age we have only one meaning for each single word. Problems arose because our parents knew us to be bright for our age and therefore expected more from us than we could produce. They wanted us to think and perform as if we were a much older child or an adult.

We were safe if we did things repeatedly and correctly. However, with all that pressure we were stressed and frightened. When we tried over and over, we failed. As a result we gave ourselves a suggestion to protect our individuality. Intuitively we were aware they wanted everything done perfectly regardless of whether or not the situation called for such preciseness. To get approval, we gave ourselves the directive to finish everything perfectly. To this day no amount of reasoning or logic can dissuade us in our effort to perform perfectly. This endless effort comes from the standard reality of a ~3 year-old child, who absolutely chooses to continue to seek comfort only with the normal behavior of an infant regardless of the situation.

All our actions in this regard will be at a level of the two year old. Our reality is that of a functional two year-old. Each time we attempt to function as an adult will cause us continuous stress. We are dysfunctional.

This example is just one of the common causes of human STRESS. That is, the ongoing contest between the subconscious mind's reality and the conscious mind's reality.

Another example is the behavior of an alcoholic. This is very readily understood because of the stress that he was under, and was revealed during hypno-analysis.

Many alcoholics are very good in the work that they do. However the stress work causes is severe. This stress originated at 30 months of age as a reaction to his family's pressure to force him to compete with his father and siblings. At that point he developed a protective hang up to resist this pressure and stay at a normal 30 month old behavior where he felt competent.

As an adult he found that alcohol made him very comfortable. The more he drank in the morning the more he was relieved of the pressure of pretending to be an adult. As he drank, he increasingly lost control and could return functionality to the safe state that he had at the 30 month-old level. When he played in the sandbox (bar) he found others with similar infantile behavior and then they could all enjoy together.

Doing this he lost all of his concern about others and only enjoyed life with his 2 year-old behavior. Alcohol allowed his infant and adult behavior to become the same and he therefore felt more comfortable drunk.

Section 2   BELIEF SYSTEM FORMATION

As human beings we have a brain that is more highly developed than any other animal in this world. One of the unique features of the marvelous brain is awareness of time and of occurrences at any moment. We also have a sense of what is right for us at that moment. This ability of assessing what is advantageous for us grows incrementally as we age. As a fetus, newborn, infant, child and adult up to senility, we gain more wisdom. At any time of life, with the diverse experiences of living and the challenges to our individuality, we often form a defense. All defenses become part of our belief system.

Living matter, from the tiniest virus to the human being, forms a defense when attacked or challenged. Humans form these defenses by creating an image to counter or avoid these diverse threats. The sophistication of these defenses is determined by the state of evolution of the individual's brain and nervous system at the moment of theat.

Always the defense is logical and realistic to the subconscious mind in its state of development at that instant. Each defense becomes registered for the lifetime. If this occurrence provokes only a little emotion, it will be hard to recall. However, if there are high emotions at that moment, defenses, images, and beliefs formed at that instant will control behavior for the rest of one's life. We can very temporarily exert conscious control over their expression but never expunge them. Training therapy, in which we create alternative images of behavior, can give us an alternative to choose more adult action.

If a person is behaving childishly or holds on to a belief that has no relation to reality then they have reverted back to reenacting the behavior appropriate to a childish belief. If behavior has no reality or logic for the immediate present, then the action is being directed by programs created by the emotionally immature brain and nervous system. In this state of mind no one will listen to or tolerate any adult thought, or consider change.

In conclusion, every belief, defensive action and prejudice is always normal, logical and realistic when placed it the original subconscious emotional context in which the individual formed it.

Section 3   CREATE AN ALTERNATE HARD DRIVE

The subconscious mind is like the hard drive in a computer. Our programming comes formatted with our DNA. It is the basic operating system for our brain. Even before birth it began to function and after birth it is continuously developing to upgrade our fundamental operating system. With exposure to an emotional experience we learn to create an added permanent inscribed record. These learned responses may be favorable and supportive or stifling for our ability to cope with the future and the current realities. These learned added behaviors are registered, to never to be erased.

We record and inscribe experiences attended with high emotions with a much deeper inscription than those of passive occurrences. Seldom will we become aware or more than temporarily conscious of these learning experiences.

It is important to recognize that defenses learned in the first three years of our life's experience are there forever and automatically and continually control our beliefs and behavior. We can use our conscious mind to willfully override most of these subconsciously directed learned behaviors. With continuous effort we can temporarily force a more mature behavior that is in line with reality. Continuous overriding of these subconscious behaviors by forcing unreal expectations is the chief cause of stress and tension. That is, our pretending to be more mature than we feel ourself to be.

Incidentally, that is why alcohol which dulls our ability to pretend to be more grown-up and responsible, is so relaxing.

There is a huge difference between control and manage. The conscious mind only temporarily controls our thinking and behavior. The subconscious mind constantly manages 90 to 95 % of the functions of our internal organs, coordinates attitude, beliefs and all our muscle fibers to regulate smooth action. The millions and millions of communications and computations serve to operate our total mind and body is fabulous. We manage these computations simply by the use of our conscious mind to create imagery for what we want our subconscious mind to do for us.

Our mind is truly wonderful with its almost limitless capacity. Today's personal computers are miraculous but at this stage in their development are now not equal to the human brain. Most computers have a singe operating system—Apple, Microsoft or Linux. Our brains are capable of operating simultaneously two or more types of hard drive. We want our brain to have two very separate operating systems. I choose the name of the original operating system as REALITY-AMNESTY and the second REALITY-DEVELOPING.

REALITY-AMNESTY: Because the inscriptions that direct aptitude and behavior were adopted from birth and represent all of the past, they depict our life when our grasp of reality was limited. Now we can increasingly understand these and grant ourselves amnesty for believing as an infant or child, as we did at those former times.

REALITY-DEVELOPING: Because now, by the use of repeated vivid imagery for programming, we can continuously upgrade our second hard drive. This active imagery will automatically manage our present and future beliefs. These imaged pictures and activities are those that we know or feel to be entirely in accord with our current grasp of reality. From this time forward we will have a choice of believing as a child or believing and performing as an adult. This is a form of self-hypnosis.

All hypnosis is self-hypnosis. We give ourselves strong suggestions by the use of imagery. In our conscious mind we see and depict each activity to be in process and accomplished. All emotional hang-ups we developed in the past were to protect one's individuality from harm, especially from the encroachment by other people. For example, "I will never again let any person every get emotionally close to me." Or "I will never get on high places ever again [therefore I will keep from falling]."

We have the capability of creating this second and alternative hard drive. This second hard drive is complete with our DNA formatting, exactly like our original inborn hard drive for the management of our subconscious mind. Now and forever after, we will have a conscious choice of either the original hard drive or our reality-developing hard drive. This alternate hard drive will direct our desirable new beliefs and behaviors.

This new hard drive is an exact clone of our prenatal self and we will only inscribe thoughtful imagery that will support our individuality so we feel ourselves to be in mature realistic behavior. This plan is to support a new program that features us with the self-esteem of an entirely self accepting individual. Now as an adult with worldly awareness that we previously lacked, we can select a current plan rather than be directed by the previous program that was forced upon us by our caretakers.

Section 4   ANGER ANALYSIS

The key to solving any problem is to seek understanding of its purpose and its resulting product. Anger is a feeling and behavior resulting from an inborn instinct coded in the DNA for the survival of a person, and more especially for survival of his individuality. It includes a driving expectation for its fulfillment.

While in the uterus we have an ideal environment. We are gravity supported and have intimate touching of our skin with lining of the womb. There we are warm and ideally nourished for our development into a unique individual.

At birth we are quite quickly separated from our total support system and threatened with death if these supports these are not felt renewed within our new environment. Our inborn expectations will be alerted and be converted to crying in anger for reestablishment of support.

In this modern age we have refined physical procedures for life support. However, for emotional support there is a vital need for intimacy and bonding with all those people present in our environment.

As a newborn our brain and nervous systems are not yet

organized to have mature judgment and the discretionary powers of an adult. Our actions are directed entirely by inborn programming.

The automatic response for support is the cry of anger. If that brings relief and works much of time, we learn a rewarding behavior. The problem is this learning is etched deeply in the subconscious mind and cannot be easily erased. We can learn alternate behavior programming, enabling us to voluntarily choose to override this original hang-up. This is the option that we must appreciate consciously.

Our willful commands are not only useless but their stimulation makes the subconscious mind more challenged and therefore always causes the anger hang-up to be more deeply entrenched. Willful conscious thought intensifies unwanted sub-conscious automatic action. Moreover, all conscious commands are completely gone in a matter of minutes.

Theoretically, reprogramming the subconscious is simple and straightforward. Our conscious mind, except for a very few minutes, cannot abort behavioral programming. We can however MANAGE the subconscious mind. This is done by conjuring vivid sensory imagery of the final task completed. Our subconscious mind has fabulous capability to supply the millions and millions of details needed for image completion. Anyone who has ever had a complex dream knows this is entirely true.

How To Abort Anger

Pay attention to your feelings. Choose to keep anger from automatically making you think and behave as an infant. See, feel and assume yourself walking in someone else's shoes - the shoe's of the proverbial wise man at the top of the mountain with all understanding. You are clear of any thoughts of magic or fantasy and are totally realistic with the laws of the universe.

Just as you have learned thousands of tasks in the past - to drive your automobile, to brush your teeth, to jump and to play the violin - you are permanently learning a subconscious new Engram for automatic behavior--If you choose.

Remember how many times you, as a student driver, had to drive your car before it became semi-automatic.

Consider 2000 times a day flashing on a key word like MATURE to recall your image of yourself in your new shoes.

Every one of our hang-ups is an age-dated functioning Engram from the early years of our life and can be revised to coincide with our fully adult present reality.

Section 5   SIN RECONSIDERED

There are several definitions for sin in the dictionary and the most germane is, "a transgression of a religious or moral law, especially when deliberate". To use this definition we need to arbitrarily choose a determining authority.

I suggest that the ultimate authority is the Great Creator of the Universe. This is the force which gave us the complete blueprints for each individual human being, that is, unique DNA (except for an identical twin). Every person has DNA to direct him toward his ultimate development. These directions are complete and specific for our highest physical, mental and emotional attainment. Unless there is some interfering block, each human, by design, will be driven to be the best they can ultimately be. There are many contingencies that can interfere with this attainable potential however.

Interruptions in emotional development most often are generated by caretakers who impose misguided standards on their children out of "good intentions". Parents and others impose standards on children for the presumed future benefit of preventing the young from developing the very defects against which the caretakers themselves are constantly struggling.

These defects are consistently those learned behaviors which interfere with the adults' own emotional maturity. With their very determined attitude and missionary zeal for conversion, parents intrude and insist that the only proper programming is their handed-down emotional guidance. They feel that this programming is necessary and must replace the divine inscription for emotional development already embedded in their infant's DNA.

From time immemorial and from generation to generation the misuse of formative guidance has been passed down from our ancestors. This standard practice of imposing hackney beliefs on the young perpetually misdirects human emotional development. Parents imposed beliefs discourage and supplant their child's inborn DNA blueprint. This delays and destroys a child's unique individuality, especially in the first two years of life. Truly this is quite unintentional yet it creates a child with limited emotional reactions for the rest of his or her life. This is the origin of infantile or childish behavior that manifests as the Engrams, the learned and permanently inscribed templates of actions and beliefs lodged in the subconscious mind. Their effect is the learned incessant recurrence of acting out immature drives and behaviors that we recognize as emotional hang-ups.

The most fundamental tenant in human life is individuality; that NOBODY HAS RIGHTS IN YOU and YOU HAVE NO RIGHTS IN ANY OTHER PERSON. Rights in any other individual result in slavery. In every day life many people, by mutual agreement, accept this slavery to a certain degree rather than live true freedom.

Each person must be the most important person unto himself. Also each person must understand and accept that no other person may consider him as important. Sustaining individuality is the very basis of human morality.

Reality

Reality is not a new religion but simple acknowledgment that the universe is as it is, including all its highly designed and functioning systems such as laws of physics, chemistry, gravity, electronic forces, time, space and all its other features functioning uniformly for 15 billion years. In Reality there can never be compromise, revenge, favorites, exceptions or singularities.

Today in the light of ever increasing knowledge and understanding about the everlasting immutable laws of physics, I find it impossible to believe in any form of magic or miracle. With current knowledge most spectacular occurrences of the past can now be understood. In the future, all details of every event will be found to comply with the orderly universe.

Prayer has an important place in everyday activities - not to get especial attention from the Great Creator for our begging to him to alter his whole universe to grant us, the practitioner, or a nation a special capricious dispensation or favor, but rather for we alone to revise our personal EXPECTATIONS. We need to make all of our expectations conform entirely to the reality of this instant. To be an emotionally fully developed adult, we need to accept the reality of this very moment and every person as he is right now. To wish any of it to be different will, with certainty, cause us personal misery and hell on earth.

Meaningful prayer avoids attempts to change anyone's behavior or judgment , including our own, but rather only intends to adjust our personal expectations to be realistic. Accordingly we need to grant amnesty for everyone's emotional behavior. We can do so when we realize that their acting-out of childish behavior is a very necessary protective device originating in response to their parent's attempts to control them. They are repeating patterned behavior or Engrams learned as an infant or child, which denies their individuality. Much of our emotional behavior was a protective response to our parent's controlling precepts and examples. We need to change our expectations and accept only beliefs and behaviors that are in keeping with our realistic adult emotional maturity. With concerted action we will be able to manage conscious imagery and create new Engrams to fulfill the inborn directives of our DNA.

Personal prayer requires that we recognize that everything is governed by the rules of eternity as it is, always right now, in other words, Reality.

The Great Creator designs each element of the universe to be logical, consistent and constant. Our whole life as humans is tremendously involved with interpersonal relationships. The Great

Creator designed and established in every person and in each cell of the body DNA whose expression mandates our individuality. Furthermore each unit of human DNA has its own set of pathways for development into mental, physical and emotional aspects.

Keep in mind that a newborn human infant is a very emotionally primitive animal. He is dedicated only to himself and his most basic drive is to stay alive. His nervous system is in place but full development and maturation is years away. His nerves have only rudimentary neuronal sheaths to insulate one from another. Only a fraction of his neuronal synapses are formed and functioning. An infant cannot have adult understanding, advanced morality, sense of responsibility or mature love. Infants under the age of thirty-six months are incapable of understanding responsibility and therefore have no conscience.

Currently moralists unconditionally condemn as "sin" behaviors such as total self-interest, anger, covetousness, slough, uncontrolled soiling, greed etcetera. An adult considers all these actions and behaviors to be sinful. In general almost all acts and behaviors that adults label as "sinful" are in reality *normal behavior* of infants and or small children. These same infantile or childish behaviors enacted by a chronologically older child or adult are labeled "sin". You might therefore consider the morality of infants as Original Sin.

Explosive anger and total selfishness in an adult are examples of a stunted emotional infant's hang-ups. This undeveloped emotional infantile or childish behavior has been created by his caretaker's "good intentions" in a misguided effort to protect their child.

In reality the Great Creator has no chosen people. All sins are transgressions against the expression of mature individuality.

The very best medicine is preventive. Especially important is prevention of emotional immaturity. The whole mechanism of developing emotional hang-ups can be prevented by the simple technique of treating the infant as an equal from the instant of birth and constantly continuing this attitude forever thereafter. Consider infants as individuals with severe handicaps of intellectual and emotional development, but vital potential for development.

The opposite of Individuality and Reality is Social Justice (socialism, oligarchy, communism, Obamaism etc.). In all of these organized social systems there is the precept and purpose that all individuals who work and earn for their own good need to be forced by law to share their goods and gains. With socialism the individual is a nothing, so his goods must be confiscated as public property. Accordingly all materials are property of the ruling class and must be distributed (theoretically equally) to those who cannot, or by choice will not, produce and save goods or wealth for themselves. Since recorded time every one of these systems of social justice have failed. Historically the evolutionary law of nature "survival of the fittest" has endured everlastingly. No governing set of rules can change this universal law.

Each and every emotional hang-up keeps us from being a distinct and   separate individual. That is, our available responses are governed by the programs installed into us by our caretakers. This in turn prevents us from using our present mature emotional expression, the drive for emotional maturity ingrained in our DNA.

Consider the thought that every domestic disagreement and discord has a common basic problem. That is, one or the other persons in a dispute attempts to forcefully control another's individuality to conform to their wants. Instead of managing their own separateness, one or both individuals are attempting to force control over the other individual. These actions represent their will to deny and prevent the other person's expression of his or her individuality. We are not required to listen to or approve the Engrams of the other person, however, there is a dire need for we to recognize, accommodate, and grant amnesty and respect to the other person's drive underlying his immature position and attitude. In doing so we need never compromise our own integrity as an individual. For example, we play make believe with our two year old daughter. We allow and encourage her to play out any fantasy she wishes. If we at that time of life treat her as an equal, that attitude will allow her to emotionally mature, because she will later recognize facts from fiction.

If an adult believes in "fantasy", he has a severe emotional hang-up.

Today to "be saved from sin" means only one thing. That is, revising the Engrams in the subconscious mind. These are recorded subconsciously as the active functioning emotional attitudes, beliefs, and actions of infancy and childhood. These initial Engrams need to be countered by new adult Engrams in order to have the free choice for adult beliefs and actions. With consciously contrived imagery we create these alternate adult Engrams. With constant repetition we generate lifelong new directions for our subconscious mind. Cease all attempts to use logical direction or attempts to order our subconscious mind. Control is not only entirely ineffective for anything more than a few minutes but also supports and strengthens our repeating those former behavior Engrams of childish and infantile origin. Conscious control is only good for minutes whereas subconscious management by imagery can be effective for a life time. To rescue and save ourselves from sin demands that we know about the workings of the subconscious mind.

Section 6   THE WORKINGS OF THE SUBCONSCIOUS MIND

Ninety to ninety-five percent of everything that we know, move, believe and do is managed automatically by our subconscious mind. We construct consciously a live image of the task that we want our subconscious mind to actively accomplish. The subconscious mind adds the millions of details to accomplish it. Part of the time it does so immediately but often it requires hours of practice to learn. Any lasting change is these activities can only be accomplished by revision in the programming of our subconscious mind.

I similarly to most all other human beings had assumed that by using my homo supine superior intellect. I could consciously and willfully change programming by negating and expunging part of my working subconscious inscriptions. Exactly the reverse is true. My calling attention to my assumed defect served only to further solidify and intensify my unwanted behavior. This processing is called imaging. It is the only way of directing subconscious behavior. There are no negatives in the subconscious mind. No one ever can draw an image of "not doing" something.

When I simply identify any pattern, I know that it is impossible or nearly so to change a set behavior. To have me or a well-meaning parent order that I immediately stop and desist a destructive activity, serves only to solidify and perpetuate my learned habitual response.

The working of the subconscious mind is essential to the structure of my belief system and it's aligning my attitude and my whole life.

All living matter—viruses, amoeba, lower animals, human beings—have inborn defenses and mechanisms, for example the immune system, to adapt to a changing environment and new challenges.

We have a second defense system to protect our separate individuality (soul) from losing our personal unique identity. This is all learned from exposure to other people whose efforts are to extinguish our identity and impose their own prejudice. These learned defenses, all subconscious, constitute probably seventy percent of our total defenses.   They are all focused on prevention of encroaches by other people.

The conscious mind is very limited. At any one time, it can only keep one to three thoughts under control and this control is limited to minutes. There can be several consecutive repeats but no permanent change. As soon as my concentration is lost the subconscious mind resumes its former steady management.

Expectations determine our attitude. Attitude determines our quality of life. When our expectations are in total accord with current reality life will be peaceful, pleasant and rewarding. If any part of our expectations is not in accord with current reality, We will create a varying amount of discontent and misery for ourselves. Here is why one problem arises. As our emotional mind continues to evolve after birth, added information stimulates advanced concepts of reality and these continually enlarge as we mature. At one year of age our concept and ability to conceive reality and consider our place in this world and society was totally apart from the future learned and experienced life as adult of thirty. At a very early age our semi-permanent defenses automatically develop to protect our individuality from our caretaker's determination to inflict their programming into our normal developing separateness. At age one year our as a result of our defense routine, we did lock-in beliefs that remain fixed for the rest of our life. These beliefs will always be infantile. Our assumptions were and are realistic and fine when we were 12 months old. However, when we compulsively use these infantile defenses at age thirty, we am out of reality. Our behavior for us and others around us will always cause all of us to suffer miserable consequences. "Act your age." Aren't you ever going to grow up?"

When factually we are emotionally mature, we will be free of these infantile and childish "hang-ups". We will be totally out of reality to expect change in ourselves, or that another person give up his life-defensive infantile or childish behavior for this is emotionally impossible to do. The only remedy is creating a dual supportive program so that we can forever choose which of the two we want. This substitute must be a positive alternative scripting in our automatic subconscious belief system. The only alternative for us is positively creating and practicing, like learning to play the piano, the imaging of a second program.   Also be advised that by insisting that we must not "do that' (naming the behavior) will, in fact, make our disgusting behavior even stronger and more resistant to change.

Probably the hardest reality to accept is that we generate and are totally responsible for our own emotions. We create the milieu for emotional expression by our own EXPECTATIONS. Nobody does anything any thing to us but project their images for us and their immediate or future behavior, which causes us to respond emotionally. When we accept their projected active images as fact, they control us. To ignore and resist, we almost simultaneously need to understand the reality of each encounter and call up our own subconscious program that sustains our personal identity. If we instantly react to their projected images, then both of us are out of reality.   When we accommodate their expectations, then we will always have immediate personal misery. Once again we alone are responsible for our own emotional well being. We must know ourselves whom we are, better than anyone else.

Section 7   Summary Points

- Wisdom is soundness of decision and action, and is inherent in our DNA.

- Full expression of our genetic potential is the state of the savant – non-judgemental understanding and acceptance of reality.

- The full expression of our genetic potential is blocked when, in childhood, we adopt emotionally charged beliefs as a defense of our personal identity from the assault of our caretakers.

- Our degree of limitation and stress is:
                    <u>Reality of us as a savant</u>
                    Reality of our childish beliefs

- Acting out subconscious emotional patterns results in dedicating our logical thinking conscious mind to defending our position and precludes wisdom.

- To acquire wisdom, all beliefs need to become temporary assumptions.

- We must choose to repeatedly engage in creative imagery to form new templates of emotional response to give us new mature behavior options

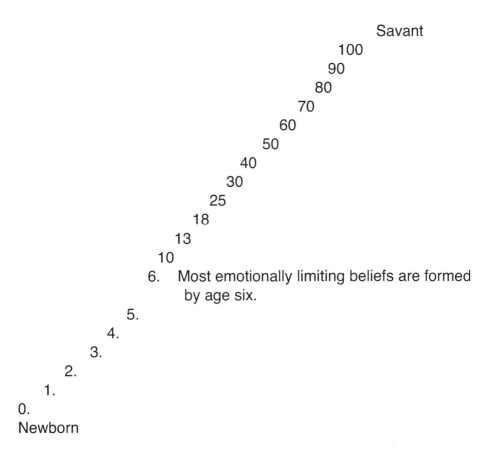

Savant

100

90

80

70

60

50

40

30

25

18

13

10

6.   Most emotionally limiting beliefs are formed by age six.

5.

4.

3.

2.

1.

0.

Newborn

Section 8   APPLICATION OF SMITH PSYCHOLOGY

The natural inborn drive of each humans is to fully develop the potential of his DNA. Any individual can be readily analyzed as to how far advanced they are toward this emotional goal by simple analysis. The analysis starts with observing a person's behavior since any infantile or childish behavior indicates emotional hang-ups. All immature behavior is less than adult behavior for it is a belief adopted in early life. Each hang-up is totally joined with an immature sense of reality. Each persisting childish behavior is an absolute block to wisdom. For example extreme anger is appropriate in a small baby who feels his life is threatened. The baby's reality is threatened with death. Extreme anger can never occur in a totally mature adult.

A totally wise person would realize that anger for himself or any other person would accomplish nothing but stress upon himself.

A further example is bullying which is a three to four year old activity wherein a child who feels incapable of competency and is fearful and attempts to denigrate a supposed competitor.

Bullying is often displayed by a politician who fears his inadequacy and has little confidence in his own ability. Consequently he attempts to denigrate his opponent. This politician is totally devoid of wisdom for the rest of his life in this special area. This special area is common to a three or four year old child.

These blocks do not necessarily interfere with intellectual maturity but do interfere with a sense of morality

Any person who has multiple intransient beliefs and does not reprogram his subconscious mind to form more adult beliefs can never be a wise mature adult individual.

Self Analysis

If you ever feel you should make any excuse for your or any other person's immature beliefs or behavior, than you are part of the problem. This belief comes with a childish sense of Reality and obscures further wisdom in this area.

You will never learn everything about anything. All belief needs to be open ended.

When you activate your behavior to execute one of your beliefs your thinking critical thinking mind is suspended in order to defend all your effort in defense of your prejudice. This exercise further increases your resolve in the Engram lodged in your subconscious mind.

The old saw "birds of a feather flock together" is exemplified in mob action by those who join a riot. Each riot gives the opportunity to activate the terrible infantile anger and the retaliation that they temporally hold in suspension at other times.

There is no magic is the huge vote that get a person elected. The candidates identify with the general population. Many people feel that acting with any immature behavior like lying in anger is entirely justified. They vote for the candidate that is most like themselves.

Section 9   THE EMOTIONAL AROUSAL LOCUS IN THE BRAIN

Keeping "in touch' is a life essential for a human being. It is it is the fourth essential after the need for air, water and food. Intimate association with another person is best understood by the communication of touch. There are no substitutes for these essential needs.

An example for this need of relationship is in obesity, wherein an attempted substitute is an over-distended stomach. This is an attempt at satisfaction to replace a lack of intimacy and nearness "being in touch".

Our body's integument comprises skin, hair and nails which combined make the largest organ of our body.   Our skin has very sensitive nerve receptors in every square millimeter of surface. Each receptor is joined to a specialized nerve fiber. These fibers are part of afferent pain and light touch nerves. They end in specific areas of the brain. I name one of these the *Emotional Arousal Locus*, the mechanism of which is similar to that of the "itch" locus. This is a special center in the brain to modulate interpersonal relationships. I label this as the "*Smith Emotional Arousal Locus*". The exact anatomical location I will leave up to the researchers in neuroanatomy.

The existence of this locus is very easy to demonstrate to yourself, on your own body. By applying the lightest touch possible or even the warmth of your hand in proximity over your face, hair, or through your clothing, you will stimulate your brain. Light touch is far different from rubbing, massage or hugging. These receptors excite special emotional afferent sensory fibers to the central nervous system. They end in a specific area of the brain that is dedicated to the integration of emotional responses. These neural transmissions are quite similar to the reception of the itch stimulation, that end in a definable locus.

We first experienced "being in touch" when we were in our mother's womb. We still need these sensations to continuously feel interpersonal associations for the rest of our life. The universal need is evident always. If fellow humans are not available animals can be substituted, but do not truly replace humans.

I have witnessed how a mother cow immediately after the birth of her calf, licks her newborn all over to establish continuous intimacy and association with the herd.

Humans are equipped with sensory organs that keep us in touch and oriented with the universe physically. Our five senses and their variations maintain this constant relationship. We have two additional senses that are not often recognized. These are attitude and expectations.

We have only limited ability to modulate the reception of the usual five senses. However with attitude and expectations we have 100% control of our perception over these vital two. This unique ability is of the upmost importance because this ability gives us complete and sole dominance over our whole quality of life.

Nobody can make us feel anything. Our attitude toward what another person is saying or doing determines entirely what we feel. Our expectations determine what emotions we perceive. Our expectations need to be realistic because what is certainly going to happen will happen. If we are always saying and expect something entirely impossible or unlikely to occur, then we must always suffer the resulting feeling consequences. There are very few statements you can say with absolute certainty but this is one of them.

Additional notes on stroking:

There are multiple practitioners available to give us touching, and animals to exchange petting.   Man's best friends are dogs. That is because universally dogs are the animals who are the most needy to share strokes.

After the age of 80 and forty years of single person investigation, I found the key to unlocking and understanding the mechanism of intimacy.

Here are instructions for the renewal and expression of mutual intimacy, especially for those over sixty.

The Practice of Being In Touch

After you have practiced very light touching on your self, then begin very slowly giving this stimulation to your mate. The ultimate for interpersonal intimacy is to daily set time aside for at least 15 to 30 minutes to experience very, very light strokes over your partner. Begin to touch gradually over her body. Later she will return this touching. After a long interlude, you might discover that she would find it agreeable for you to gently slip your hand inside of her clothing, and so on.

I tell my women patients that should they become a widow, there is almost 100% of men who have not truly been stroked since infancy. She can interest almost any man she wants if she starts stroking almost imperceptibly and systematically.

REFERENCES

The information in this paper is the accumulated insight of thirty years of independent research by the author using his simple technique of Age Reenactment Hypnosis to explore the subconscious mind.

Related books by Dr. Theodore J. Smith:

Full Share

Kinship and the Dark Side of Man

Made in the USA
San Bernardino, CA
29 March 2014